The Civil War

PETER BENOIT

Children's Press®
An Imprint of Scholastic Inc.
New York Toronto London Auckland Sydney
Mexico City New Delhi Hong Kong
Danbury, Connecticut

Content Consultant
James Marten, PhD
Professor and Chair, History Department
Marquette University
Milwaukee, Wisconsin

Library of Congress Cataloging-in-Publication Data

Benoit, Peter, 1955–
  The Civil War/Peter Benoit.
      p. cm.—(A true book)
  Includes bibliographical references and index.
   ISBN-13: 978-0-531-26309-9 (lib. bdg.)   ISBN-10: 0-531-26309-6 (lib. bdg.)
   ISBN-13: 978-0-531-26622-9 (pbk.)   ISBN-10: 0-531-26622-2 (pbk.)
   1. United States—History—Civil War, 1861–1865—Juvenile literature.
I. Title.
  E468.B46 2011
  973.7—dc22   2011012047

All rights reserved. Published in 2012 by Children's Press, an imprint of Scholastic Inc.
Printed in China 62
SCHOLASTIC, CHILDREN'S PRESS, A TRUE BOOK, and associated logos are trademarks and/or registered trademarks of Scholastic Inc.
1 2 3 4 5 6 7 8 9 10 R 21 20 19 18 17 16 15 14 13 12

Find the Truth!

Everything you are about to read is true *except* for one of the sentences on this page.

Which one is **TRUE**?

T or F The Battle of Gettysburg was the bloodiest battle of the Civil War.

T or F President Abraham Lincoln was assassinated before the Civil War.

Find the answers in this book.

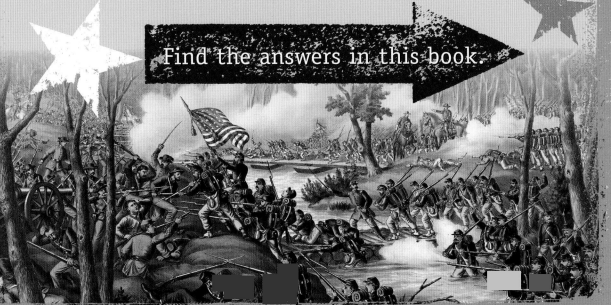

5

Contents

THE **BIG** TRUTH!

The Battle of Gettysburg

Union army leaders

General Grant's Union army blocks railroads and burns farms.

4 The Aftermath

5 Lasting Effects

General William Tecumseh Sherman has been called the first modern general.

Cotton growers shipped their products out from port cities such as New Orleans, Louisiana.

CHAPTER 1

Reasons for War

The United States was broken into two separate nations from 1861 to 1865. They battled one another in a **civil war**. The years leading up to the war were filled with bitter conflict. Much of the southern states' economy depended on growing and **exporting** cotton. But the South lagged behind in industrial development despite its strength in agriculture. Instead, it purchased goods from northern states or from Europe.

In the mid-1800s, three-quarters of the world's cotton was grown in the southern United States.

By 1860, there were four million slaves living in North America.

Some southerners fled to the North because they disagreed with southern beliefs.

The Strength of the South

Wealthy southern plantation owners had controlled national politics before the war. The U.S. Congress and the Supreme Court were controlled by men who supported the South's political and economic interests. The southern economy relied on enslaved Africans to provide labor. Slavery was not allowed in most northern states. In part this was because it was largely unnecessary in an economy that was based on manufacturing.

New Taxes

Northern manufacturers found it difficult to compete against less expensive imported goods from Europe in 1828. To help them, Congress placed a tariff, or tax, on imports. Southerners believed that this pressured Americans to purchase goods from the northern states. They thought European manufacturers might lose money and purchase less cotton from the South.

Southerns were angry. They felt that the tariff was helpful only to northern states.

Northern businesses manufactured a wide variety of goods.

The U.S. government lowered the tariff rate in 1832. But many southerners were not satisfied. South Carolina passed a law to end the tariff in the state. It also threatened to **secede** from the Union if it were forced to pay the tariff. Other states did not support South Carolina. It was soon forced to give up the fight against the tariff. But its actions planted the seeds of secession in the southern states.

The idea of nullification was developed by Vice President John C. Calhoun.

John Calhoun published two books containing his ideas about government.

Mobs of angry slaveholders often broke up abolitionist meetings.

Growing Problems

The differences between the North and South continued to grow. The issue of slavery became a bitterly divisive national concern. Northern **abolitionists** argued against slavery on moral grounds. Some openly encouraged slaves to rebel against their owners. Despite this, most northern citizens did not wish to end slavery. They simply wished to prevent its spread. One of the men who took this position was a politician from Illinois named Abraham Lincoln.

The Slavery Debate

Slavery was one of the most heated issues in the country in the years before the Civil War. Regions being settled in the West, such as Utah and New Mexico, had recently become territories of the United States. There was much debate over whether or not to allow slavery in these new areas. Many southerners believed that slavery should be guaranteed in all territories. They thought that slavery should not be outlawed in these areas unless they became states and decided it for themselves.

Secessionists created a special flag representing support for states' rights.

South Carolina's secession encouraged other states to secede.

The Beginning of War

Southern politicians feared the end of slavery was near when Lincoln won the 1860 presidential election. Most believed he was an abolitionist. They wished to preserve slavery and their states' rights to make decisions for themselves. Some believed that the only way to do this was to secede. South Carolina became the first state to secede from the Union on December 20, 1860. Mississippi, Florida, Alabama, Georgia, Louisiana, and Texas followed in the next six weeks.

Delegates from the seven states met in February 1861 to form a new nation called the **Confederate** States of America. They chose a former U.S. senator named Jefferson Davis as their president. They also drafted a Confederate constitution that upheld slavery. The Confederacy printed its own money, established its own Congress, and created its own flag. The Confederacy allowed individual states more power than the United States did. It did not even have a supreme court. It instead encouraged states to govern themselves.

Davis served as secretary of war under President Franklin Pierce.

Jefferson Davis was the first and only Confederate president.

The first shots of the Civil War were fired at Fort Sumter in South Carolina.

U.S. troops at Fort Sumter in South Carolina sent word that they needed supplies in spring 1861. The fort was one of the only Union-controlled military bases left in Confederate territory. President Lincoln agreed to send the supplies. He notified South Carolina of his intent. But the Confederates feared that Lincoln would also send weapons and troops. Confederate soldiers fired on Fort Sumter, beginning the American Civil War on April 12, 1861.

Union soldiers fire on pro-Confederate rioters in the streets of Baltimore, Maryland.

CHAPTER 2

A Bloody Conflict

President Lincoln called on state **militias** to defend federal forts and Washington, D.C., after the attack on Fort Sumter Virginia, Tennessee, North Carolina, and Arkansas then joined the Confederacy. A militia responding to Lincoln's request was attacked in Baltimore, Maryland, by Confederate sympathizers. More than a dozen people were killed by the angry mob. Lincoln had the mayor and city council arrested.

Historians consider the Baltimore Riots the first bloodshed of the Civil War.

Cutting Off the South

The Union decided to weaken the Confederacy with a **blockade**. Unable to export cotton, the Confederacy would have a hard time funding the war. Lincoln warned British and French leaders that supporting the Confederacy would lead to war with the United States.

This map shows the Union and Confederate states during the Civil War (1861–1865).

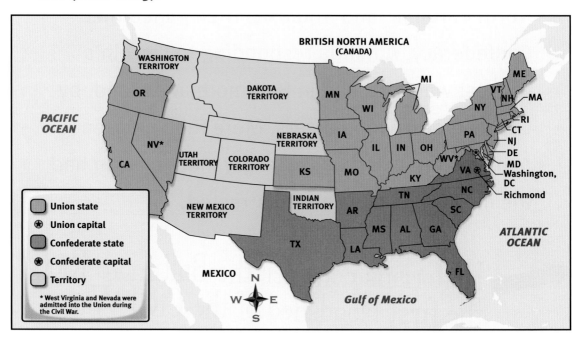

24,000 Union and Confederate troops were injured or killed at Bull Run.

Thomas "Stonewall" Jackson was one of the most successful Confederate generals during the Civil War.

Confederate Victories

The Confederates fought well against the Union during the first year of the war. Confederate General Thomas Jonathan "Stonewall" Jackson earned his nickname in July 1861. He held back the advancing Union army at Bull Run, Virginia. The Confederates won another major victory on June 1, 1862. Jackson and General James Longstreet defeated Union commander George McClellan at the Battle of Seven Pines. This victory prevented the Union forces from capturing the Confederate capital at Richmond, Virginia.

Confederate troops often had to deal with supply shortages.

Economic Pressure

The blockade was beginning to wear down the
Confederacy by 1862. Union forces began to gain
control of waterways and railways in the South.
They also took food from Southern farms while
fighting there. Food shortages became common in
the Southern states. Both armies began requiring
young men to join. The Union's larger population and
economic strength began to turn the war in its favor.

The Battle of Antietam

Confederate general Robert E. Lee pushed successfully into Union territory in the summer of 1862. His goal was to draw Union troops away from the Confederate forces in Virginia. On September 17, Union commander George McClellan met Lee's forces near Antietam Creek in Maryland. Losses were heavy on both sides. The Confederacy lost 13,724 troops and the Union 12,410. The Union was victorious. Lee was forced back to Virginia.

The Battle of Antietam is also known as the Battle of Sharpsburg.

President Lincoln met with General McClellan and his men after the Battle of Antietam.

The Emancipation Proclamation

President Lincoln was encouraged by the victory at Antietam. He issued the **Emancipation Proclamation** on January 1, 1863. This proclamation announced that all slaves in the Confederacy were considered free by

With one document, President Lincoln freed all of the slaves in the Confederacy.

the U.S. government. The proclamation did not free slaves in border states such as Maryland because they were still part of the Union. But it was an important step toward ending slavery completely.

Almost 30,000 men were killed or injured at the Battle of Chancellorsville.

Wounded soldiers often did not receive good medical care.

The Battle of Chancellorsville

General Lee's forces in Virginia were camped across the Rappahannock River from Union general Joseph Hooker throughout winter 1862. Hooker attempted to circle around Lee's forces and prevent a retreat in late April 1863. But on May 2, Lee ordered General Jackson to sneak around to the Union's side. The Confederates achieved victory. But they suffered a major loss. In addition to more than 12,000 casualties, Jackson soon died of injuries he suffered during the Battle of Chancellorsville.

The Battle of Gettysburg

General Lee's army clashed with the forces of U.S. general George Meade at the town of Gettysburg, Pennsylvania, on July 1, 1863. The two sides fought the single bloodiest battle of the entire war for three days. More than 51,000 troops from the two armies were killed, injured, or missing. Lee was forced to retreat back to the South. It would be the last battle fought on Northern soil. Many consider it to be a major turning point for the war. President Lincoln gave a speech, remembered as the Gettysburg Address, several months later at the battleground. Lincoln's inspiring words stressed the importance of reuniting the country.

July 1

The outnumbered Union forces make a strategic retreat to the high ground of Cemetery Ridge, to the south of Gettysburg. More Union forces join them at night.

July 2

Both sides suffer heavy losses throughout the day, but the Union maintains the advantage of its higher ground. Union forces fight back Confederate attacks at Little Round Top and the Peach Orchard.

July 3

Lee attempts to make a massive attack on the center of the Union forces in what became known as Pickett's Charge. This decision ends up costing Lee the battle, as the charging Confederates are wiped out.

The Siege of Vicksburg

The Union scored another major victory just one day after Gettysburg. Its forces had been attempting for months to take the Confederate city of Vicksburg, Mississippi. Vicksburg was located along the Mississippi River. Controlling it would prevent communication between the main Confederate forces and their allies in the west. It would also improve Union communication along the river. Union general Ulysses S. Grant surrounded the city on May 18, 1863. He prevented any supplies from going in. Vicksburg was forced to surrender by July 4.

Grant's leadership helped the Union win many battles.

Grant's Plan

President Lincoln placed Grant in charge of the entire Union force in 1864. The general soon created a plan to destroy the remaining Confederate forces. He planned to block railroads and burn farms to keep the Confederates from resupplying. The blockade was also still going strong. Many necessary goods were scarce. This caused severe **inflation**. The costs of countless products skyrocketed.

General Grant's strategies were successful in helping to ruin the Confederate economy.

Wilderness and Spotsylvania

General Grant and his 115,000-man army began a campaign to take the Confederate capital city of Richmond in 1864. Grant met Lee's forces in a thickly wooded area near Fredericksburg in early May. Grant moved onward after two days of fighting. The following day, Grant and Lee clashed once again at Spotsylvania Court House. They fought for 11 days before Grant once again moved his troops forward toward Richmond.

Nearly 40,000 men were killed, injured, or missing after the Battle of Spotsylvania Court House in Virginia.

William Sherman was named Tecumseh after a well-known leader of the Shawnee people.

General Sherman and his men left a trail of destruction as they made their way to Savannah.

"The March to the Sea"

Grant worked closely with General William Tecumseh Sherman throughout the last half of the war. Sherman captured the major Confederate city of Atlanta, Georgia, on Septebmer 2, 1864. Soon after, he and his 62,000 troops began the "March to the Sea" as they headed toward the coastal city of Savannah. They destroyed railroads, farms, and other Confederate resources along the way.

The Final Battles

The Confederates still held the capital city of Richmond at the end of 1864. But they were low on food and supplies. They were also heavily outnumbered. Grant began the final push to victory in spring 1865. The Union won the Battle of Fort Stedman in March. This reduced Lee's army to just 50,000 men. Grant scored another victory for the Union at the Battle of Five Forks on April 1.

The Union saw victory at Fort Stedman in Virginia.

Appomattox Court House became a national historical monument in 1940.

Lee's surrender brought an end to the Civil War.

The End of the War

Lee advised that Richmond be evacuated after the Battle of Five Forks. Confederate president Jefferson Davis fled to Danville, Virginia. Lee's forces were surrounded at the town of Appomattox, Virginia, on April 9, 1865. Lee surrendered to General Grant that day at Appomattox Court House. This all but ended the war, though some Confederates continued fighting until May. More than 620,000 people had died in the four-year war. Many of them were very young. Great damage had been done to the South. It would take years to recover.

President Lincoln was in the presidential box at Ford's Theatre when he was shot.

CHAPTER 3

The Aftermath

On April 14, just days after Lee's surrender to Grant, President Lincoln attended a play at Ford's Theatre in Washington, D.C. Lincoln's bodyguard left his post during a pause in the performance. A pro-Confederate actor named John Wilkes Booth sneaked into the balcony where President Lincoln and his wife were seated. Booth fired a single bullet into Lincoln's head from close range. The president died early the next morning.

 John Wilkes Booth was a successful Shakespearean actor.

Abraham Lincoln

Abraham Lincoln was born in a rural area of Kentucky on February 12, 1809. He had little formal schooling. But he read whatever books he could find. After a short time in the Illinois militia, Lincoln entered politics in 1834. He served first in the Illinois state **legislature** and later in the U.S. House of Representatives. In 1860, he was elected president. The North and South were already bitterly divided when he took office. Lincoln saw his highest duty as preserving the Union. His leadership during the Civil War helped earn him a place in history as one of the greatest presidents the country has ever seen.

Rumors spread that Booth was not actually the man killed at the Virginia farm.

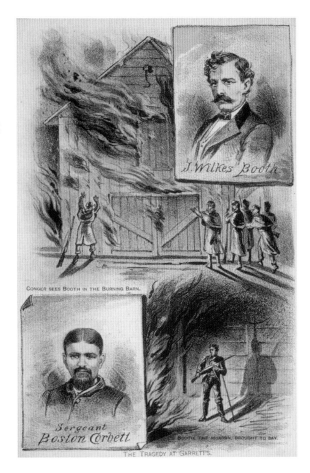

J. Wilkes Booth

CONGER SEES BOOTH IN THE BURNING BARN.

Sergeant Boston Corbett

BOOTH THE ASSASSIN, BROUGHT TO BAY.

THE TRAGEDY AT GARRETT'S.

Booth refused to surrender even after the barn he was hiding in caught fire.

Booth escaped from the theater, but police hunted for him. Federal agents found him hiding in a barn at a Virginia farm on April 26. He refused to surrender and was shot. Booth had not planned the **assassination** by himself.

35

Partners in Crime

Booth had planned his attack with several other people. They originally planned to kill other important leaders such as General Grant and Vice President Andrew Johnson at the same time. But these attacks failed. In addition to Booth, seven men and one woman were tried for planning Lincoln's murder. Four were hanged. One died in prison. The other three were pardoned by President Johnson.

Timeline of the Civil War

December 20, 1860
South Carolina secedes from the Union.

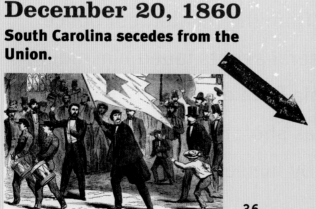

April 12, 1861
Confederate forces fire on Fort Sumter, beginning the Civil War.

The Fate of Jefferson Davis

Jefferson Davis was captured near the town of Irwinville, Georgia, on May 10. He was immediately put in prison. He was freed without being tried for treason (helping the enemy during war) two years later. Some historians believe that Davis was never tried because the U.S. government feared that he would win in court. This would have proved that the Southern states had seceded legally. Davis never regained his U.S. citizenship.

July 1–3, 1863
The Battle of Gettysburg is fought.

April 9, 1865
Lee surrenders to Grant at Appomattox Court House.

Lincoln spoke often of his belief in the importance of unity among the states.

CHAPTER 4

Lasting Effects

President Lincoln gave a famous speech in 1858, before he was elected President. He said in it that the United States could not "endure, permanently, half slave and half free." He issued the Emancipation Proclamation using the special war powers of the presidency five years later. But the proclamation did not end slavery for good. It would take an amendment to the U.S. Constitution to permanently end slavery.

Lincoln said that he hoped white and black people "could gradually live themselves out of their old relation to each other."

Members of the U.S. House of Representatives celebrate after approving the 13th Amendment on January 31, 1865.

The 13th Amendment

Work began on the 13th Amendment to the Constitution near the end of Lincoln's first term as president. It took many months to complete. The amendment was finally approved by the states in December 1865, eight months after Lincoln's death. Slavery was formally abolished in the United States and its territories at long last.

The 14th Amendment

The 13th Amendment ended slavery. But former slaves still lacked many basic rights. Some of these rights were granted by the 14th Amendment in July 1868. This amendment extended the definition of a U.S. citizen to be anyone "born or naturalized in the United States." It also ensured the benefits of life, liberty, and property to all citizens, as well as the right to a fair trial.

The 14th Amendment made it illegal for former Confederate leaders to hold public office.

Former slaves worked hard to establish new lives as free people.

The first black congressman was elected less than a month after the 15th Amendment was ratified.

Former slaves began voting and running for office almost immediately after the 15th Amendment was ratified by the states.

The Fight for Equality

Many African Americans faced unfair treatment even after the 13th and 14th Amendments. The 15th Amendment gave African American men the right to vote in 1870. But African Americans faced discrimination for another hundred years. This discrimination was especially bad in the South. In some ways, the fight for true equality continues even today, but it began with the Civil War. ★

True Statistics

Confederate losses at the Battle of Antietam: 13,724

Union losses at the Battle of Antietam: 12,410

Number of Confederate soldiers killed or injured at the Battle of Gettysburg: About 24,500

Number of Union soldiers killed or injured at the Battle of Gettysburg: About 23,000

Total number of soldiers who fought in the Civil War: About 2.4 million

Number of soldiers killed during the Civil War: More than 620,000

Did you find the truth?

T The Battle of Gettysburg was the bloodiest battle of the Civil War.

F President Abraham Lincoln was assassinated before the Civil War.

Resources

Books

Aretha, David. *Jefferson Davis*. New York: Chelsea House, 2009.

Benoit, Peter. *The Confederate States of America*. New York: Children's Press, 2012.

Benoit, Peter. *Abraham Lincoln*. New York: Children's Press, 2012.

Junyk, Myra. *The 10 Most Defining Moments of the Civil War Era*. New York: Children's Press, 2008.

Kent, Zachary. *The Civil War: From Fort Sumter to Appomattox*. Berkeley Heights, NJ: Enslow, 2011.

Koestler-Grack, Rachel. *Abraham Lincoln*. New York: Chelsea House, 2009.

McNeese, Tim. *Civil War Leaders*. New York: Chelsea House, 2009.

Sheinkin, Steve. *Two Miserable Presidents*. New York: Roaring Brook Press, 2008.

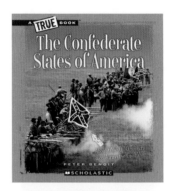

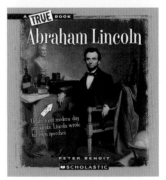

Organizations and Web Sites

Library of Congress—Time Line of the Civil War

memory.loc.gov/ammem/cwphtml/tl1861.html
Take a year-by-year journey through Civil War action, with detailed explanations and photos of all the key moments of the conflict.

PBS—The Civil War

www.pbs.org/civilwar
On the official site of the award-winning documentary, *The Civil War*, by Ken Burns, you can explore Civil War photographs, battle maps, biographies, historical documents, and much more.

Places to Visit

Gettysburg National Military Park

1195 Baltimore Pike, Suite 100
Gettysburg, PA 17325
(717) 334-1124 ext. 8023
www.nps.gov/gett/index.htm
Take a guided tour of the Civil War's bloodiest battle site, and relive the sense of danger experienced by soldiers on both sides.

Lincoln Memorial

National Mall and Memorial Parks
900 Ohio Drive SW
Washington, DC 20024
(202) 426-6841
www.nps.gov/linc/index.htm
Visit this inspiring monument and learn about its construction and significance as a symbol of hope and freedom.

Important Words

abolitionists (ab-uh-LISH-uh-nistz)—people who worked to end slavery permanently

assassination (uh-sas-uh-NAY-shuhn)—the murder of someone well known

blockade (blah-KADE)—a closing off of an area to keep supplies from going in or out

civil war (SIV-uhl WAR)—a war fought between residents of the same country

confederate (kuhn-FED-ur-it)—belonging to a union of people or nations

Emancipation Proclamation (uh-man-sih-PAY-shuhn prah-klu-MAY-shuhn)—the statement issued by President Lincoln that freed all slaves in Confederate states.

exporting (EK-sport-eng)—sending products to another country

inflation (in-FLAY-shuhn)—a general increase in prices

legislature (LEJ-is-lay-chur)—a group of people who have the power to make or change laws

militias (muh-LISH-uhz)—groups of people who are trained to fight but who aren't professional soldiers

secede (si-SEED)—to withdraw formally from a group or an organization

strategic (struh-TEE-jik)—carefully considered as part of a plan for winning a military battle or achieving a goal

Index

Page numbers in **bold** indicate illustrations

About the Author

Peter Benoit is educated as a mathematician but has many other interests. He has taught and tutored high school and college students for many years, mostly in math and science. He also runs summer workshops for writers and students of literature. Mr. Benoit has also written more than 2,000 poems. His life has been one committed to learning. He lives in Greenwich, New York.

10